ESSENTIAL TIPS

101

REMOVING STAINS

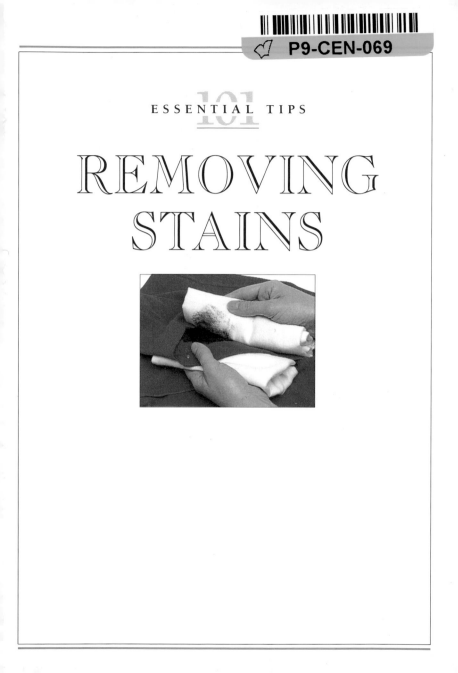

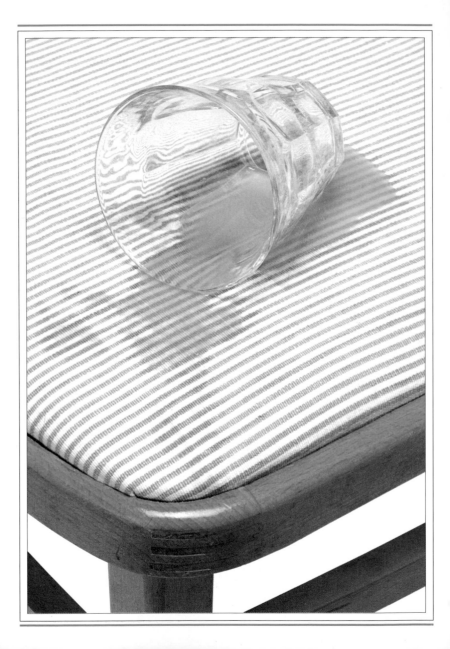

ESSENTIAL TIPS

REMOVING STAINS

Cassandra Kent

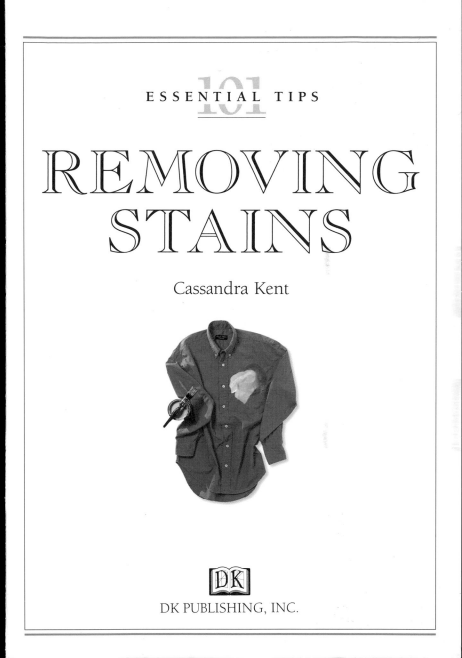

DK
DK PUBLISHING, INC.

A DK PUBLISHING BOOK

Editor Bella Pringle
Art Editor Gill Della Casa
DTP Designer Robert Campbell
Series Editor Gillian Roberts
Series Art Editor Clive Hayball
Production Controller Lauren Britton
US Editor Laaren Brown

First American Edition, 1997
2 4 6 8 10 9 7 5 3
Published in the United States by DK Publishing, Inc.
95 Madison Avenue, New York, New York 10016

Visit us on the World Wide Web at http://www.dk.com

A catalog record for this book is available from the Library of Congress.

ISBN 0-7894-1459-7

Text film output by The Right Type, Great Britain
Reproduced by Colourscan, Singapore
Printed and bound in Italy by Graphicom

ESSENTIAL TIPS

—————— PAGES 28-30 ——————

BATHROOM FIXTURES

—————— PAGES 31-36 ——————

KITCHEN EQUIPMENT

—————— PAGES 37-41 ——————

FURNITURE & BOOKS

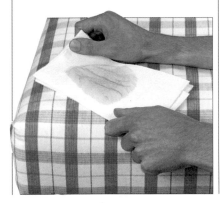

ESSENTIAL KNOW-HOW

1 HOW TO TREAT STAINS

The secret of successful stain removal is to treat the stained item at once. Stains that have time to soak in and dry are very difficult to remove and, in some cases, leave a permanent mark. Illustrated below are a few common "stainers" that you may encounter.

RED WINE ▷
A full glass is easily knocked over onto carpets, table linen, upholstered furniture, and clothing, so get to know the best treatment for each of these items.

FELT-TIP PEN △
Children find it hard to resist drawing on walls and furniture, and pens left in jacket pockets often leak.

FLOWER POLLEN ▷
Dusty orange pollen can be picked up on clothing if you brush past lilies.

◁ YOLK OF EGG
Runny yolk of egg that has dripped onto clothing and table linen forms a crusty deposit if not dealt with at once.

2 DIFFERENT TYPES OF STAIN

Although stains can be divided into broad categories, depending on whether they are built-up deposits, absorbed, or ground in, the same rules apply to all. Before tackling any type of stain, consider the surface on which it has fallen, and any special dye, treatment, or finish on that surface. Whatever the type of stain, you must test your method of stain removal on a hidden area first, to check that your treatment is not going to make matters worse.

△ BUILT-UP STAINS
These are made by thick substances, such as ketchup and paint. They leave a surface deposit but do not penetrate far.

△ ABSORBED STAINS
These are spilled liquids such as ink, fruit juice, wine, and coffee that have been absorbed into fabric or carpet fibers.

△ GROUND-IN STAINS
These dried or set stains are caused by foods or mud that have been either sat on or carried around on footwear.

3 TREATING "MYSTERY" STAINS

If you cannot identify the cause of a stain, proceed with caution by choosing a mild method of stain removal. Soak washable items at once, and then wash according to care instructions. Nonwashable items should be gently dabbed with a sponge wrung out in warm water.

4 STAIN-REMOVAL EQUIPMENT

The illustrated collection of items shows the basic equipment you will need to tackle household stains. Organize a stain-removal kit to keep these cleaners and solvents handy. Then you will be able to act quickly if accidents happen. When blotting stains or applying solvents, always use white paper towels and cloths to avoid any transfer of dye.

COTTON BALLS ▽

△ BROWN PAPER

△ PAPER TOWELS

◁ WHITE CLOTHS

△ COTTON SWABS

△ SPONGE

△ SPOON

RUBBER GLOVES ▷

△ DENATURED ALCOHOL

△ RUG SHAMPOO

△ GLYCERIN

△ LEMON

△ EUCALYPTUS OIL

△ LAUNDRY BORAX

△ POWDERED DETERGENT

△ TALCUM POWDER

HARD FLOORS

STUBBORN MARKS ON VINYL

Although most spills are simple to wipe off vinyl, scuff and heel marks cause permanent damage. Most scuffing occurs when kitchen appliances are dragged in or out of their allocated space, so be careful. To remove marks, dip a soft white cloth in turpentine and work in circular motions. Rubbing the area with an eraser may also work.

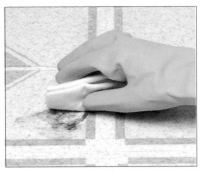

RUB VIGOROUSLY TO DISSIPATE THE MARK

6 BURN MARKS ON VINYL & CORK

Accidental burns on vinyl and cork floors are common, especially if you light the gas stove with a match. If the floor has been laid as tiles, just replace one, but for sheet vinyl, try these solutions.

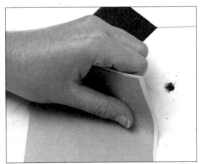

SANDPAPERING MINOR BURN MARKS
To remove light burn marks from vinyl and cork, rub the damaged area with a folded-over sheet of fine-grade sandpaper.

CUTTING OUT SERIOUS MARKS
If a burn is serious, use a craft knife and a metal ruler to cut out a square of vinyl around the mark. Then insert a new piece.

7 SCUFF MARKS ON LINOLEUM

Linoleum, like vinyl, is prone to scuffing. To protect kitchen and bathroom floors and other wet areas from surface damage, polish them regularly with an emulsion polish – being water-based, it will not leave watermarks. Use a wax polish on other linoleum floors. If scuff marks do occur, rub them until they disappear with fine-grade steel wool dipped in turpentine.

GENTLE ABRASION REMOVES SCUFFS

8 STAINS ON UNVARNISHED WOOD

Natural stripped-wood floors are hygienic and easily maintained, but because unsealed wood is very absorbent, liquid stains can seep into the grain. Act quickly to avoid serious staining and then – for a longer-term solution – seal the floor permanently with polyurethane.

1 Mop up the spill with paper towels and then, wearing heavy-duty rubber gloves, sponge the stain with a solution of bleach until the color lifts. Finally, wash the area with detergent solution.

2 When the stained area has dried out, the floor is ready to seal. Apply the polyurethane with a medium-sized paint brush, following the direction of the grain. Several coats may be needed.

9 SCRATCHES ON VARNISHED WOOD

Although well-protected from stains, varnished wood floors are susceptible to scratching, especially if furniture is dragged rather than lifted across a room. To avoid having to replace a section of the floor, which can be costly, follow this two-step repair technique.

1 Wearing rubber gloves, gently rub the scratch with fine-grade steel wool to smooth it out. Be careful to follow the line of the scratch so as not to damage a larger area of flooring.

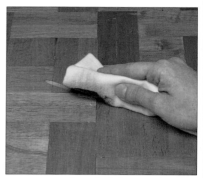

2 Mix together a little brown shoe polish and floor wax. Apply the mixture to the scratch on a soft cloth. Rub in well until it masks the scratch and blends in with the rest of the floor.

10 INK ON WOOD FLOORS

Fountain-pen ink can be difficult to remove, especially if it is an old stain that has gone unnoticed. With a cotton swab, gently dab the ink with undiluted household bleach. Blot with paper towels, and repeat if necessary. Always use quick dabs of bleach because rubbing the area will leave white spots on the wood. For a large spill, strip off surface layers of varnish and treat the stain with a commercial wood bleach.

11 CANDLE WAX

If hot wax drips onto your wood floor, suspend a plastic bag filled with ice cubes over the wax to harden it. When it has set solid, ease off the wax with a blunt knife or a similar tool. When all the deposit has been lifted, rub the wood with a soft cloth to remove any film. Next, apply a little liquid floor polish to your cloth and buff well. Where heat marks have also occurred, rub along the grain with cream metal polish (Tip 58).

12 MARKS ON FLOOR TILES

Ceramic tiles usually resist staining and simply need regular cleaning with a hot solution of dishwashing liquid. Never apply polish since this makes the ceramic slippery. Unglazed terra-cotta tiles can be scrubbed with water and a liquid all-purpose cleanser, and then polished with paste wax. Stone tiles respond best to a detergent solution, but they should be sealed.

△ **REMOVING WHITE PATCHES**
Sponge a solution of 4 tbsp vinegar to 5 quarts (5 liters) water over tiles to prevent lime from seeping up through the concrete subfloor.

STONE FLOORS ▽
Most stone floor tiles are sealed and therefore quite difficult to stain. Clean dirty grouting with a soft bristle brush (Tip 37).

Ceramic tiles *are the most impermeable of all floor materials.*

Marble tiles *can stain on contact with food acids.*

Slate *is durable, water-resistant, and hard to stain.*

CARPETS & RUGS

13 DEALING WITH SPILLS

The secret of stain removal from carpets is to treat food and drink spills while they are fresh, and always to work from the outside to the middle of the stain to avoid spreading it further. Dab the area gently rather than rubbing it, and never use hot water or the mark will set. Stains on carpets are divided into two main types: built-up stains and absorbed stains; some stubborn stains, such as congealed blood and egg, are a combination of the two types.

△ SCRAPING OFF BUILT-UP STAINS
Built-up stains are produced by thick substances that need to be scraped off before the carpet can be treated. Scoop them up quickly to prevent absorption.

△ ABSORBING LIQUID STAINS
Thin liquids will sink quickly into the carpet surface. Blot the area at once with layers of white paper towels to absorb most of the stain before further treatment.

△ TREATING THE REMAINING MARK
After removing any built-up or liquid deposit, treat the remaining mark with rug shampoo. If this leaves an obviously clean spot, shampoo the entire carpet.

14 FOOD STAINS ON CARPETS

Carpet is one of the most expensive items in the home to replace, so consult the treatment chart below to help you remove some of the typical colored food stains that befall carpeted areas.

YOLK OF EGG
Scrape up the egg with a blunt knife, and apply a commercial liquid stain remover on a white cloth to tackle any remaining mark. If the stain is still visible when dry, sponge on a solution of rug shampoo, but try to avoid overwetting the carpet.

MUSTARD
Scoop up the deposit, and sponge the area with a mild detergent solution. If any color remains, apply a weak ammonia solution made from 1 tsp to 2 cups (500ml) cold water.

TOMATO SAUCE
Scoop up the deposit. Sponge the area with clean warm water; blot dry. Apply a lather of rug shampoo and wipe off. When dry, spray with aerosol stain remover if needed.

DARK-COLORED FRUITS
Pick up squashed fruit, and absorb any juice with paper towels. Rub the area with laundry prewash stick. A few minutes later, rinse it off, blot dry, and then shampoo.

CURRY & CURRIED SAUCES
Wipe up the curry and dab the area with laundry borax solution – 1 tbsp 2 cups (500ml) warm water – or rub glycerin into the pile.

CHOCOLATE
Leave the chocolate to set, then scrape it off. Apply a lather of rug shampoo, and wipe well. When dry, use a liquid stain remover.

BEETS
Do not attempt to remove beet juice from carpets or rugs. Have wall-to-wall carpets professionally cleaned in the home, and take rugs to a specialist dry cleaner.

JAM & JELLY
Scrape off the surface deposit with a spoon. Dab the area, using warm water to get rid of any stickiness, then treat the stain with rug shampoo. Remove any residual marks with denatured alcohol.

15 GREASY FOOD ON CARPETS

Foods such as mayonnaise, butter, salad dressing, cream, ice cream, and gravy may land on carpets during meals. They contain oil or fat and tend to leave behind a greasy patch if not properly treated.

The secret of successful stain removal is first to absorb as much of the grease as you can from the carpet before tackling the food coloring: oily beauty products and lotions, and traces of car oil on carpets should be dealt with in the same way. Follow this three-step treatment to remove both minor and major stains from carpet pile.

1 △ If the substance is thick, first scrape up as much of the deposit as you can, and then blot the area with paper towels. If only a light mark remains, apply a commercial stain remover. For heavier deposits, go to the next step.

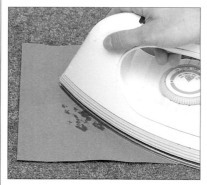

2 △ Place a piece of brown paper, dull side down, over the grease patch. Apply the tip of a warm iron to loosen the grease. As the brown paper absorbs the grease, move it around to the next clean area until no more grease lifts off. Be careful not to let the iron come into contact with the carpet or it may scorch.

3 △ If any grease marks remain, use a sponge to apply a lather of rug shampoo. Rub the carpet gently but firmly for a few minutes. Wipe off the foam with a clean cloth. If any evidence of grease is still visible or reappears at a later date (as sometimes happens), repeat the application of rug shampoo.

16 DRINK STAINS ON CARPETS

Liquid spills are rapidly absorbed into carpet fibers, so try to act quickly for best results. After treatment, smooth down the carpet pile in the direction in which it lies, and leave to dry out naturally.

TEA
Fresh spills should be blotted and then flushed out with a soda syphon or sponged with warm water. For tea containing milk, use rug shampoo and, when dry, apply an aerosol stain remover.

BLACK COFFEE
Fresh black coffee stains may be treated in exactly the same way as black tea: absorb the liquid with paper towels, then dilute the coloring with warm water.

BEER
Fresh beer stains can be treated as for black tea and coffee, but remove old stains by carefully sponging the mark with turpentine.

HARD LIQUOR
Flush away fresh stains from hard liquor with soda water or sponge with warm water. Then blot well with paper towels. Stubborn stains need to be treated with rug shampoo, and old stains respond to turpentine.

FORTIFIED WINES & LIQUEURS
These produce highly colored, stickier stains than other alcoholic drinks. Dilute the stain with warm water and blot. Apply rug shampoo. Treat residual marks with stain remover.

FRUIT JUICE
Act with speed: fruit juice can leave a permanent mark. Soak up the liquid with paper towels, then rub the area with a commercial stain-removing bar before shampooing. Lift final traces with turpentine.

MILK
The smell of sour milk can linger if it seeps in, so take quick action. Sponge with warm water and, when dry, apply an aerosol cleanser.

MILKY COFFEE & COCOA
These stains are a mix of coloring and grease. First sponge with tepid water, then apply rug shampoo. When dry, use a liquid stain remover.

17 RED WINE ON CARPETS

Red wine spills are perhaps the most common of carpet stains. The best quick response is to pour white wine over the area: contrary to popular belief, this is much more effective than sprinkling the stain with salt. Then, continue with the process described in these steps.

2 △ Blot the mixture of wines with white paper towels, pressing down on the carpet pile to squeeze out as much of the liquid that has been absorbed as possible.

1 △ If you happen to have a glass of white wine at hand, pour this over the red wine as soon as the spill occurs. Make sure that you cover the area.

4 △ If the stain is particularly stubborn, cover any traces with glycerin diluted with equal parts of warm water. Leave for an hour to loosen the mark. Sponge off with clear water. Blot dry.

3 △ Sponge the stained area repeatedly with clear warm water. Blot dry, and then rub in the foam from some made-up rug shampoo. Rinse off with clear warm water. Repeat until the stain lifts.

18 HOUSEHOLD PRODUCT STAINS

The average home contains an assortment of chemicals in quite ordinary substances like medicines, cosmetics, and glues as well as cleaning products. Many of these can produce colored stains, which are tricky to remove, once trapped in carpet fibers. Follow this guide explaining how best to treat some familiar household "stainers."

SHOE POLISH

Have everyone clean their shoes on old newspaper, but if polish gets on carpet, scrape off what you can. Remove any traces with turpentine, and then rinse with clear warm water.

MEDICINES

Treat sticky medicines with rug shampoo, but iodine like this. Buy hyposulfate (a chemical used to develop photographs). Dilute ½ tsp in 1 cup (250ml) warm water and sponge the mark. Finish off with rug shampoo.

CANDLE WAX

Colored candles may leave dye stains on carpets, but these can be successfully treated with denatured alcohol. First scrape off the wax deposit, then melt any leftover wax particles with a warm iron placed over a piece of brown paper (Tip 15).

METAL POLISH

Do try to avoid polishing metal objects in parts of your home that are carpeted, but if polish happens to spill, scoop up as much liquid as you can, and blot at once to prevent absorption. Dab the area with turpentine, and let it dry naturally. When the area has thoroughly dried out, a stiff brush will remove any powdery residue. Apply rug shampoo afterward if necessary.

NAIL POLISH & LIPSTICK

Blot up as much as possible with white paper tissues. Apply nonoily nail-polish remover on a cotton ball to the area, but first test a hidden section of carpet since the rubber backing may be damaged if solvent soaks through. Apply denatured alcohol to traces of color that remain, then treat the area with rug shampoo.

CREOSOTE & TAR

These sticky black marks are difficult to lift once caught up in carpet fibers. Scrape off any deposit, and then loosen with equal parts glycerin and warm water. Leave for an hour and rinse. When dry, use stain remover. Eucalyptus oil rubbed into the pile can also work.

COLORED PLASTIC PUTTY

Children's modeling clay can easily be ground into carpets. Lift off as much of the deposit as possible with a blunt knife. On small areas, dab with lighter fluid, but test a hidden area first. Use stain remover on extensive marks.

FOUNTAIN-PEN INK

Even so-called "washable" ink requires special treatment. First dilute the stain by sponging with clear warm water, and then blot dry. Dab on a warm solution of liquid soap on a folded piece of white fabric, working it in for about 15 minutes. Repeat until the stain disappears; blot well between applications. Rinse with clear water. Finish by blotting dry.

FELT-TIP PEN

Fast action is needed to stop colored ink from soaking in. Blot small marks with cotton swabs and more serious leaks with paper towels. Use denatured alcohol to remove color from small areas. Larger stains need aerosol stain remover.

CHEWING GUM

Hold a plastic bag filled with ice cubes over the tacky chewing gum to harden it. Using your fingernails, crack and pick off the hard gum. Apply a commercial liquid stain remover to any remains, and sponge the treated area with warm water.

Chewing gum sticks like glue to shoes and fabrics

Treat before carpet fibers are permanently damaged

19 NEW & OLD PAINT STAINS ON CARPETS

Even if you take great care to cover up your carpets with old cloths when painting, paint may still accidentally seep through and stain the carpet underneath. (It is often not until the end of the day that you discover a paint stain – by which time it has probably dried.) These solutions will help achieve the satisfactory removal of new and old marks created by latex and oil-based household paints.

LATEX PAINT
Treat paint that is still wet by sponging with cold water. Try to avoid spreading the stain further. Loosen dried paint with denatured alcohol but perform a color test first. When clear, apply rug shampoo.

GLOSS & OIL-BASED PAINT
Blot wet paint with paper towels and treat with rug shampoo. For old stains, try using a commercial solvent, after an initial test. If this does not break down the stain, use scissors to snip just the top of the pile.

Nail scissors allow delicate snipping

SNIP OFF DAMAGED CARPET FIBERS

20 GLUE ON CARPETS

Apply glue sparingly and wipe away the surplus while it is wet, to prevent accidental spills. Water-based glues become water-resistant once they have set, while rubber-based glues may respond to lighter fluid. Often the best solution is to cut dried glue off the carpet pile.

21 SCORCH MARKS ON CARPETS

A smoldering cigarette or hot coal falling out of a fireplace may burn carpet. Minor scorches can be rubbed away with sandpaper, but a badly burned patch needs to be replaced with a matching remnant.

1 Place a matching section of carpet over the badly burned area, and cut both layers together with a craft knife.

2 Fit the new piece of carpet into the space. Secure it in position using strong double-sided adhesive tape.

22 TREATING BIOLOGICAL STAINS

Biological stains on carpets are often spread by pets and should be treated immediately for reasons of hygiene. Urine, vomit, and feces also have unpleasant odors that will only increase if left to linger.

URINE
Treat pet stains with a deodorizing carpet cleaner, or sponge with cold water and blot. Apply rug shampoo. Rinse with cold water and a few drops of antiseptic.

VOMIT
Lift the deposit, and sponge the area with a laundry borax solution made from 1 tsp 2 cups (500ml) of warm water. Rinse with clear, warm water and antiseptic.

FECAL STAINS
Scrape up the feces, being careful not to spread the stain further. Gently sponge any remaining marks with a solution of warm water and a few drops of ammonia.

MUD
Leave the mud to dry for a couple of hours. Then loosen the dried mud with a stiff brush and vacuum up the deposit. Use denatured alcohol to lift stubborn traces.

BRUSH UP THE MUD WHEN DRY

WALLS, WINDOWS, & FIREPLACES

23 MARKS ON WALLPAPER

If you live in a polluted city area, or if there are smokers in the house, washable walls are a must.

For nonwashable wall coverings, localized marks can be removed by following the techniques below.

TACKLING GREASE MARKS
Place brown paper over the grease mark and press with a warm (not hot) iron. Repeat, using clean parts of the paper.

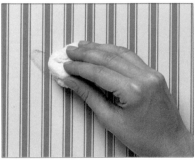

REMOVING DIRT MARKS
Gently rub away marks on wallpaper with a piece of crustless white bread scrunched up into a ball. Repeat if necessary.

24 FINGERMARKS ON PAINTED WALLS

To remove dirty fingerprints that can accumulate around heavily used areas, such as light switches, gently rub the area with an eraser. Wash food stains with undiluted, nonabrasive household cleanser.

CONCENTRATE ON ONE AREA AT A TIME

25 PEN MARKS ON WALLPAPER

In households with young children, felt-tip pen scribbles on walls can be all too common. Like ballpoint-pen marks, felt-tip pen is notoriously difficult to remove. The best solution is to cover the marks with a new piece of wallpaper, as shown in the following steps.

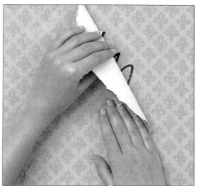

1 Badly pen-marked wallpaper may be beyond cleaning but can be easily patched if you have any spare wallpaper. Carefully tear off a matching piece from the spare roll. Do not cut it with scissors: an uneven edge produces the best result.

2 Position the new patch over the mark. When you have made sure that the pattern matches, glue it into place with wallpaper paste. When patching old paper, leave the new piece to fade in the sun to achieve a better color match.

26 TREATING MILDEW

Mildew tends to appear on cold kitchen and bathroom walls where steam condenses as water. The fungal spores appear as small dark patches, which may develop a deposit if left unchecked. Wash the whole area with a mild detergent solution. Pay special attention to the corners and window frames. Sponge the wall with a solution of commericial antibacterial soap.

27 CRAYON MARKS ON WALLS

Pencil marks can be rubbed away with an eraser, but crayon marks are impossible to remove from ordinary wallpaper. The area will need repatching, while painted walls require repainting. Scrub vinyl wallpaper with a sponge and dish-washing liquid.

28 GREASY FINGERPRINTS ON WINDOWS

Grease from our fingers and hands is quick to transfer to glass, especially around door handles. Young children and pets, who are constantly commuting between one room and another, are particular offenders. To make sure that window cleaning is not a chore, clean off marks as they occur, to avoid a build up of stubborn stains.

1 Add white vinegar to water to make your own window-cleaning solution that cuts through greasy marks. Use a plant-spray bottle to mist it onto glass.

2 Give windows an extra shine by buffing them dry with a crumpled-up sheet of newspaper. Its inky print creates that spectacular shine.

29 SMUDGE-FREE WINDOW CLEANING

Windows need regular cleaning both inside and out, and this is best done on overcast days when fingerprints and smudge marks are more easily seen on panes of glass. Windows that are washed in the sunshine will also dry too quickly, making them impossible to clean without leaving streaks.

30 FLY SPECKS ON WINDOWS

Attracted to the light, flying insects often bump into windows, leaving quite unsightly specks on the glass. When they dry out, these specks can become encrusted and difficult to remove. Treat lasting marks with denatured alcohol applied on a soft cloth so as not to scratch the glass. Remember to rub vigorously.

31 BURN MARKS ON FIREPLACES

The brickwork surrounding fireplaces needs regular cleaning, since high flames repeatedly licking the fireplace can leave behind black scorch marks. Scrub these burned areas with clean water and a stiff brush, then sponge with undiluted white vinegar and rinse well.

SCRUB HEAVY SOOT STAINS

32 SOOT MARKS ON BRICKS

Soot marks are common in homes that have fireplaces. Use the nozzle of a vacuum cleaner to suck up light marks, and scrub ingrained dirt with clean water and a stiff brush. Treat persistent stains with a weak solution of hydrochloric acid in water, but be careful since it is highly poisonous and corrosive.

33 STAINS ON MARBLE HEARTHS

Although marble is known as a hardwearing surface that is difficult to scratch, it is also fairly porous. The surface can pit and mark on contact with spilled liquids such as wine, tea, and coffee.

1 Cover the liquid stain with salt to stop it from seeping into the marble. Brush off the salt, then reapply a fresh quantity as the stain is soaked up.

2 If the liquid appears to be staining the surface, pour milk over a fresh heap of salt and leave for a few days. Wipe with a cloth wrung out in water.

BATHROOM FIXTURES

34 SCALE AROUND THE PLUG

Visible hard-water deposits tend to accumulate around drainholes of bathtubs and sinks. Hard-water deposits manifest themselves as brown unsightly patches that are difficult to remove. To restore the surface finish in the drain area, rub the deposit vigorously with the cut side of half a lemon. Alternatively, try a commercial product.

RUB WITH HALF A LEMON

LET THE NOZZLE SOAK IN VINEGAR

35 DESCALING FAUCET NOZZLES

Where hard-water deposits build up on faucet nozzles dulling their shine, you can dissolve the scale by soaking the nozzle in vinegar. To do this, fill a plastic bag with white vinegar and attach it securely onto the nozzle with string, making sure that the nozzle is immersed in the liquid. Let the nozzle soak for several hours or overnight until the scale has dissolved. Untie the bag, rinse the nozzle, and then polish to restore its brilliant shine.

36 CLEANING FAUCET BASES

Even with daily cleaning, bathroom grime and hard-water deposits can collect in the crevices around faucet bases. An old toothbrush is the ideal tool for reaching into these difficult areas. Dip the head of the toothbrush in a household cleaner, and gently scrub backward and forward around the base.

SCRUB WITH AN OLD TOOTHBRUSH

BRUSH GENTLY WITH THE SOFT BRISTLES

37 CLEANING TILE GROUTING

Grouted ceramic tiles in bathrooms and kitchens soon gather dirt along the grout crevice. This looks not just unattractive but unsanitary, too. Remove the dirt with an old toothbrush or soft-bristled brush dipped in a bleach solution. If the grout is very grubby, replacing it could be a better option.

38 SCRATCHES ON ACRYLIC TUBS

Light scratches on acrylic tubs can be rubbed away with cream metal polish on a soft cloth. For deeper scratches, smooth the surface with a fine-grade wet-and-dry abrasive paper or pad. Use the paper wet, and continue rubbing until the paper has worn down, so that you work with increasingly fine paper. Finish with a cream metal polish.

WORK WITH WET ABRASIVE PAPER

39 MILDEW ON SHOWER CURTAINS

In hot steamy bathrooms where ventilation is poor, plastic shower curtains often remain damp for some time after use. Dampness is the perfect breeding ground for mildew fungus, which appears as a dark growth of spores on the plastic curtain, making it look as though it is covered in patches of dirt. Here is how to treat mild and severe mildew.

- To remove light mildew, sponge the infected area on the curtain with a weak solution of household bleach or antiseptic.
- Heavily stained areas should be sponged down or soaked in a bleach solution, sprayed with an antibacterial agent to prevent the mildew from recurring, and hand-washed.

SOAK IN BLEACH

40 STAINS ON PORCELAIN TUBS

Different types of tubs require different care. The guide below shows how to treat stains on vitreous and enameled porcelain. Try to avoid very abrasive cleansers, which will dull the surface.

BLUE-GREEN MARKS
These are caused by the minerals in water from a dripping tap. Apply a commercial bathroom cleanser on a sponge, and concentrate on the stained area. Do not treat the stain with lemon or vinegar because they can damage the glaze.

BATHTUB RINGS
To avoid bathtub rings, remember to clean and rinse the bathtub thoroughly after use. If rings build up around the bathtub, use a bathroom cleanser and rinse well. For heavy rings, rub with a soft cloth dipped in turpentine. Rinse with a dishwashing liquid solution followed by clear water.

HARDWATER DEPOSITS
Use a bathroom cleanser on enameled porcelain surfaces. Remember that deposits show up more on dark-colored bathtubs.

RUST MARKS
Try the treatment for blue-green marks, but if this does not lift the stain, use a commercial cleanser with rust-removing properties.

Tub-cleaning equipment

KITCHEN EQUIPMENT

41 WHITENING A PORCELAIN SINK

Discoloration occurs in porcelain sinks in places where the glaze has worn down or where the surface has become scratched and dirt has collected. To restore a brilliant whiteness, arrange a thick layer of paper towels over the bottom and sides of the sink and, wearing rubber gloves, saturate the towels with household bleach. Leave for 30 minutes and then discard the towels. Rinse very well before use.

SATURATE PAPER TOWELS WITH BLEACH

42 MARKS ON PORCELAIN

Wash light markings off porcelain with undiluted liquid soap on a damp sponge, and then rinse. This method works just as well as using a commercial cleanser for tubs, sinks, and showers. Try to avoid harsh abrasive cleansers because they wear away the surface of the porcelain and make it harder to scrub clean. Stubborn marks can be removed with turpentine.

43 DULL STAINLESS-STEEL SINKS

Water splashes and fingermarks dull the finish of stainless steel. Remove water spots with rubbing alcohol or vinegar. You can restore shine by buffing with a soft cloth and stainless-steel polish.

Soft cloth will not scratch

44 STAINS ON GLASS OVEN DOORS

It's easy to spill food on oven glass, especially if your appliance has a pull-down door on which you rest hot dishes. Hot spills not wiped off at once may quickly burn and leave caked-on brown marks that are hard to remove the next day.

Wait until the oven is cold and then start to tackle the stain, using an abrasive household cleanser to wipe the surface vigorously. Clean the glass (including corners) inside and out. Finish with a soft cloth.

ALLOW THE OVEN TIME TO COOL DOWN

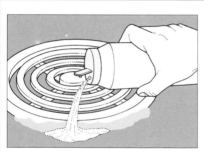

QUICK-ACTION SOLUTION

45 MARKS AROUND BURNERS

Pans bubbling away on a stove easily boil over. To prevent spills from setting, take immediate action by pouring salt over the area. Dried-on marks can be treated when the stove is cool: cover them with a cloth wrung out in detergent solution, leave for two hours, then clean.

46 BROILER PANS

Broiler pans need washing after each use to prevent a build up of fat that may catch fire. If this seems tedious, line the pan with aluminum foil before use. Then, simply discard the foil when it becomes dirty, rather than having to wash the pan every time.

LINE WITH ALUMINUM FOIL

47 POT & PAN BURNS

If you accidentally burn a pot or pan, save it in this way. Allow the burn to dry, pick off as much as possible, and then fill the pan with a solution of enzymatic detergent. Leave for a couple of hours, then bring the pan to a boil, and the deposit should start to lift. Discard the water and scrub. If the burn mark is stubborn, repeat these steps several times.

BRING THE SOAKED PAN TO A BOIL

48 ALUMINUM PANS

In time, pans manufactured from aluminum tend to discolor because of frequent contact with boiling water. To remove traces of discoloration, boil a solution of water and fruit acid from fresh rhubarb or apple peel. Rinse, then dry. To dissipate stains, soak pans in a solution of laundry borax, or add laundry borax to dishwater to act as a cleaning agent.

PREPARE A WEAK FRUIT-ACID SOLUTION

49 MARKS ON STAINLESS-STEEL PANS

Although stainless-steel pans are favored for their hard-wearing stain-resistant properties, their highly polished surface is not immune to heat or staining. Luckily, most marks can be treated.
- To remove heat marks, dip a scouring pad in lemon juice and rub in circular motions to avoid scratching the smooth pan surface.
- Use a commercial stainless-steel cleanser to lift any rainbow-colored smears caused by hot fat splashes.
- Mineral salts in tap water soon leave a white film on stainless steel. To avoid this, dry pans thoroughly.

50 BLACK STAINS ON STAINLESS STEEL

Some foods, such as egg – especially boiled egg yolk – leave black tarnish marks on stainless steel. Rub stubborn black stains on cutlery with salt applied to a damp cloth. To prevent the tarnish from recurring, always wipe your cutlery thoroughly after use.

51 PREVENTING SILVER FROM TARNISHING

Silver tarnishes easily, so it is vital to wash silver cutlery right after use. If you do not have a dishwasher, a quick way to do this after a dinner party is to put several strips of aluminum foil in a dishpan. Place the cutlery on top, and cover all the silverware with boiling water. Add 3 tbsp of baking soda, and soak the cutlery for at least 10 minutes.

SPRINKLE WITH BAKING SODA

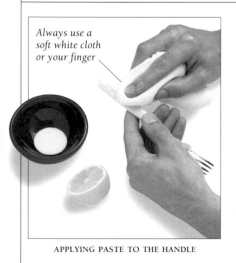

Always use a soft white cloth or your finger

APPLYING PASTE TO THE HANDLE

52 STAINS ON BONE & MOTHER-OF-PEARL

Bone and mother-of-pearl cutlery handles tend to stain yellow with age, but they cannot be washed in water because it damages them. To whiten bone and mother-of-pearl handles, mix the juice of one lemon and enough powdered tailor's chalk to make a thick paste. Use your finger or a soft white cloth to spread the paste over the handles, and leave for one hour. When the time has elapsed, use a clean, soft cloth to remove the paste from the decorative handles.

53 MARKS ON CRYSTAL & GLASSWARE

When sparkling clean, glass and crystal always look their best. To achieve a bright shine, wash delicate, tall-stemmed glasses by hand, and never put good cut glass or crystal in the dishwasher, since even gentle dishwashing soaps will eventually turn the glass cloudy.

ADDING LEMON RIND FOR SHINE
Lemon rind in the rinsing water will cut through fingermarks and food grease on glasses. Its natural acidity adds sparkle.

POLISHING TALL-STEMMED GLASSES
Make a thin paste from baking powder and water, and rub it over the glass. Rinse well and dry carefully with a soft cloth.

54 DECANTERS & PITCHERS

To thoroughly clean the insides of decanters and narrow pitchers, put in a solution of white vinegar and water and a handful of coarse sand. Shake well, and then rinse. Stubborn port stains in decanters require more drastic measures. Fill the decanter two-thirds full with a solution of household bleach, and shake from time to time to see whether the stains are lifting. Be careful to rinse the decanter thoroughly to make sure no trace or smell of bleach remains.

Hold the decanter at the neck so that you can swirl the liquid around

REMOVING STUBBORN STAINS

Gritty sand
scours vase
interior

Narrow
necked vases
are tricky to
clean inside

White
vinegar

55 STAINS INSIDE CHINA VASES

Stale flower water may stain the
inside of a vase. When the neck is
narrow, stains can be particularly
difficult to reach. To remedy
this, pour a handful of gritty
sand into the vase, then fill
with white vinegar. Shake well,
leave overnight, then rinse.

56 CLEANING THE INSIDE OF TEAPOTS

Many people just flush out
their teapot with water after use,
believing that dishwashing detergent
will affect the taste of subsequent
brews. With daily use, brown tea
stains soon build up. Follow these
steps for taste-free stain removal if
this has happened to your teapot.

1 Use baking soda to clean the inside
of a teapot, since it leaves behind no
taste or smell. Apply the powder with
a damp white cloth.

2 Rub the inside of the teapot with the
cloth, then rinse the teapot well.
Store it in a dust-free location with the
lid off to allow air to circulate inside.

57 REMOVING STAINS FROM MUGS

Tea and coffee stains on
mugs (and cigarette marks on china)
can also be removed by rubbing
with a damp cloth and baking
soda. Be careful with bone china,
as this process may dull the surface.

FURNITURE & BOOKS

58 MARKS ON SOLID WOOD FURNITURE

Furniture made from wood is very appealing, and even though most wood surfaces are protected by a coat of lacquer or wax polish, they are damaged by hot objects, water, grease, scratches, and dents.

WATERMARKS
Absorb spills quickly with paper towels to prevent the water from seeping into the wood. When dry, try smoothing out any marks by briskly rubbing cream metal polish in the direction of the wood grain. For serious marks, apply liquid wax polish on fine-grade steel wool.

GREASE MARKS
Mop up grease spills and, if a dark patch remains, wipe it over with undiluted vinegar to dissolve any absorbed grease. Then clean again with diluted vinegar.

SLIGHT BURNS
Strip away the surface finish and scrape and burnish away any rough edges. Place a soaked wad of blotting paper on top. Cover with plastic wrap. Leave overnight, then refinish the wood.

SERIOUS BURNS
Scrape out the burned wood with a sharp knife until you have a clean hole. Use a wood filler of matching color to fill in the hole. When dry, sand the filler smooth and paint on a grain to match.

HEAT MARKS
Remove white heat marks by spreading a paste of vegetable oil and salt along the grain. Leave for two hours, then wipe off.

DENTS
Treat at once by covering the hollow with damp blotting paper. Apply a warm iron on top, and allow the dented wood to swell.

SCRATCHES
Rub over the scratch with either beeswax polish and a little linseed oil, a matching wax crayon, or wax shoe polish. Buff well.

Beeswax polish and soft cloth

59 PROTECTING WOOD TABLE SURFACES

If you are planning a children's party or a large family gathering, and are anxious about damaging the surface of a high-quality wood table with food or drink spills, try the following technique.

Cover the table with a generous layer of plastic sheeting, making sure that it adheres to the table-top, and then hide the plastic layer under a decorative cloth. You can take the same preventive measure for piano tops and cocktail tables, and other pieces of furniture on which plates and glasses are likely to be set down or knocked over.

WRAP THE TABLETOP IN PLASTIC SHEETING

60 RUST ON METAL FURNITURE

Rust can be removed from metal garden furniture that has been left outside during the winter months and from indoor decorations such as a magazine rack (*see right*) by energetic scrubbing with a wire brush or steel wool. Protect your eyes from loose rust particles with goggles. If some patches are difficult to remove, treat with a liquid rust remover. To prevent further rusting, coat the item in rustproof paint or in a paste wax furniture polish.

LOOSEN RUST WITH A WIRE BRUSH

61 INK STAINS ON LEATHER

It is difficult to avoid marking a leather-topped writing desk with ballpoint-pen or fountain-pen ink. An occasional application of leather protector helps to preserve and protect the desk surface against staining. However, if stains do occur, here are two simple solutions.

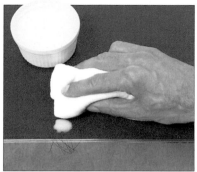

BALLPOINT-PEN INK
Treat the ink by rubbing along the length of the mark with milk applied on a soft cloth, then sponge with tepid water.

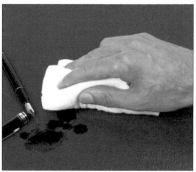

FOUNTAIN-PEN INK
Mop up ink spills immediately with paper towels to stop ink from seeping into the leather, then dab with a little turpentine.

62 TREATING IVORY PIANO KEYS

Ivory keys tend to discolor with age and regular use. To remove any mild yellow discoloration, leave the lid of the piano open on sunny days, and the sun will bleach the keys white. To clean dirty marks from ivory keys, use toothpaste on a soft, damp cloth. Gently rub one key at a time, and then rinse with milk on a cloth well wrung out to stop the milk from trickling down between the keys. Lastly, buff the keys dry with a soft cloth.

CLEANING IVORY KEYS WITH TOOTHPASTE

63 CLEANING CLOCK FACES

The case housing a kitchen clock will probably need more attention than any other clock in the house since it can soon become dulled with kitchen grease. To remove marks from the glass and the clock face, use a soft white cloth dipped in denatured alcohol. Gently wipe away any grease or grime. (Cover a valuable mantle clock with a plastic food bag for protection when doing your regular household cleaning.)

Work the cloth into all the corners

RUBBING WITH DENATURED ALCOHOL

64 MILDEW & GREASE MARKS ON BOOKS

Mildew forms when books are so tightly packed together that air cannot circulate. To discourage mildew, sprinkle the shelves with oil of cloves. To avoid grease, wash your hands before handling books.

SPRINKLE CORNSTARCH OVER MILDEW
Patches of mildew on hardback books are unsightly and, if not treated, may spread. Sprinkle the mildew with cornstarch and leave for a few days before brushing off.

First make sure the base plate is clean, and check the setting

ABSORB GREASE WITH BLOTTING PAPER
Traces of greasy food on fingers can leave marks on the pages of books. To remove grease spots, lay a sheet of blotting paper over the page and press with a warm iron.

65 MARKS ON GILT PICTURE FRAMES

Wooden picture frames covered with a thin layer of gold need special attention in order to remove stubborn marks. Warm a bottle of turpentine in a bowl of hot water and then, using a soft white cloth, rub the liquid over the frame. Clean the gilt frame with a solution of 3 tbsp vinegar in 2 cups (500ml) cold water. Polish with a soft cloth.

APPLYING WARM TURPENTINE

66 ELECTRONIC EQUIPMENT

If you tend to eat or drink at your desk, or have a telephone in the kitchen, you may find that your equipment becomes grubby. These marks and household dust are the main enemies of such equipment.

TACKLE GRIMY KEYBOARDS
Clean black marks on the tops of the keys with a supply of cotton swabs dipped in turpentine. Use dry cotton swabs to dust thoroughly between each of the keys.

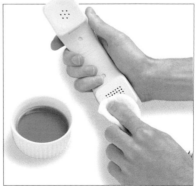

CLEAN & DISINFECT TELEPHONES
A cotton pad dipped in turpentine will clean marks off the telephone. Wipe both the ear- and mouthpieces with antiseptic fluid applied on a cotton ball.

UPHOLSTERY

67 FABRIC PROTECTION

Upholstered covers on sofas and armchairs are subjected to heavy wear, especially in homes with children and pets. Try to buy loose covers that can be regularly dry-cleaned or washed. Otherwise, protect permanent covers from stains with these methods.

◁ FABRIC-PROTECTION SPRAY
Spray newly upholstered colorfast fabrics in sweeping movements from a distance of about 8in (20cm). When dry, the spray will repel liquid so that accidental spills are easy to wipe off.

△ PROTECTION AGAINST SUN & DUST
Direct sunlight causes any fabric to fade. Protect permanent upholstery from the sun – and dust – with a washable cover.

△ PROTECTION AGAINST WEAR & TEAR
The arms of chairs and sofas are perhaps the most vulnerable areas. Guard against stains and wear with removable covers.

68 TECHNIQUES OF STAIN REMOVAL

Loose fabric covers are best dealt with according to fabric type, like all home laundry (*Tips 83–101*), but covers should be put back on while they are still damp to ensure a good fit. Permanent covers that cannot be removed should be treated by a cleaning company or with the techniques below. Test home treatments on unseen areas.

1 △ Scrape up any thick deposit, and blot the stain with white paper towels to stop it from seeping through the fabric and causing permanent damage.

2 △ If the mark has been made by greasy food or a sauce, sprinkle the area with a thick layer of talcum powder and leave until the grease is absorbed.

3 △ Wait 10 minutes, and then carefully brush away the powder with a soft bristle brush. If the mark remains, repeat the treatment with more talcum powder.

4 △ If the stain has dried, loosen it with glycerin diluted with equal parts of warm water. Rinse, then after an initial test, sponge with upholstery shampoo.

69 FOOD STAINS ON UPHOLSTERY

Meals eaten on your lap, while your attention is focused on some other activity, can increase the likelihood of food accidentally landing on upholstery. Here's how to treat some common food stains.

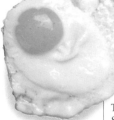

EGG
Scrape off the deposit, and sponge with cold salt water and then clear water. Use stain remover on residual marks.

YOGURT
Scoop up the spill, and sponge with clear tepid water. Blot dry with paper towels. When dry, apply an aerosol stain remover.

ALERT!
Encourage children to eat from a plate.

MUSTARD
Lift the deposit before sponging with a mild detergent solution. To remove marks, use a weak solution of 1 tsp ammonia to 2 cups (500ml) of warm water. Blot, rinse, and blot again.

TOMATO SAUCE
Scrape up the sauce, and then wipe with a clean cloth wrung out in water. When dry, use spray-on stain remover.

SOUP
Blot the spill with paper towels to stop it from seeping in. Then treat soup as for grease: sprinkle the mark with talcum powder, wait 10 minutes, then brush off. Apply upholstery shampoo, rinse, and dry.

BEETS
It is virtually impossible to remove beet stains with home treatments, so call in a home upholstery cleaner for expert advice.

JAM & JELLY
Scoop up any sticky deposit with a spoon, and then sponge on a solution of warm liquid detergent, being careful not to soak the upholstery. Sprinkle laundry borax on persistent marks, and wait 15 minutes before sponging off. Blot dry.

70 REMOVING CHOCOLATE

Dropped pieces of chocolate can cause a problem on upholstery that cannot be laundered, particularly if the chocolate gets warm and melts on the fabric, or if someone is unfortunate enough to sit on the pieces and squash them in. The following three-step technique describes the most effective way of lifting this annoying stain.

1 △ Let melted chocolate set hard, then scrape off as much of the deposit as possible with a blunt knife.

2 △ Work in a lather of carpet shampoo, rubbing gently, and being careful not to soak the cushion.

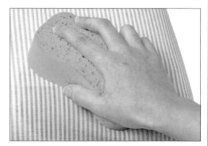

3 △ Wipe off the foam with a damp sponge. When dry, lift any traces with a liquid stain remover, after testing.

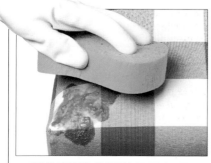

WEAR RUBBER GLOVES FOR THIS TASK

71 TREATING CURRY STAINS

Fresh curry stains are hard to get out of permanent upholstery: extensive spills may even need professional treatment. For light marks, scoop up the sauce, then rub the stain using either a cloth or sponge wrung out in laundry borax solution – 1 tbsp to 2 cups (500ml) water. Rinse and blot dry.

72 RED-WINE STAINS ON UPHOLSTERY

These steps for treating fresh stains may be less effective for dried ones, which are more difficult to remove. Quick action gives the best results.

1 △ Blot the liquid spill with absorbent paper towels. Sponge with clear warm water to dilute the stain, then blot again. Repeat if necessary. Sprinkle talcum powder over persistent marks.

2 △ Leave the talcum powder to absorb the stain for a few minutes. Clean off the powder with a soft brush, and continue the warm water and blotting treatment until the mark disappears.

73 TEA & COFFEE

A cup of tea or milky coffee resting on the arm of a chair is easy to knock off. Next time, try this tip.

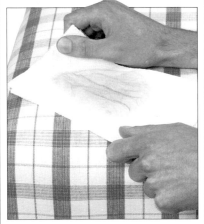

△ MILKY COFFEE STAINS
Blot the stain with paper towels, and then sprinkle with enzymatic detergent. Leave for a few minutes and wipe off.

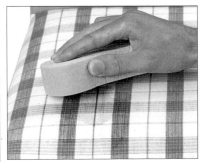

△ TEA STAINS
Sponge with laundry borax solution – 1 tbsp in 2 cups (500ml) of warm water. Wipe over with a damp cloth.

74 OTHER DRINK STAINS

When you are treating liquid stains on permanent upholstery, be careful not to soak the fabric, especially if seats are well padded, or they may take too long to dry.

MILK & CREAM
Treat at once, since these turn sour with a lingering odor when absorbed. Dab the spill with a sponge wrung out in clear tepid water. Blot dry with paper towels. When dry, use an aerosol stain remover.

BLACK COFFEE
Sponge with cold water and shampoo if need be with rug or upholstery shampoo.

HOT CHOCOLATE
Soak up most of the liquid with paper towels, then sprinkle with enzymatic detergent. Wipe off with a damp sponge.

COLA DRINKS
Blot this sticky spill with paper towels, and then repeatedly sponge the area with cold water until the stain lifts. Blot dry to remove dampness.

BEER & ALE
Blot well, then sponge the area with a clean damp cloth. Treat persistent marks with an aerosol stain remover. Sponge dried stains on natural fabrics with a mild solution of white vinegar.

HARD LIQUOR
Remove all traces of stickiness by sponging with clean warm water, then blot dry. If staining remains, use an upholstery blotting kit. With delicate fabrics, seek expert advice.

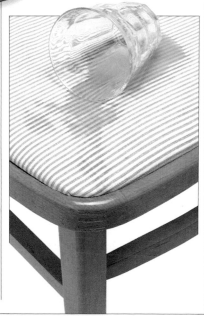

FRUIT JUICE
Sponge the fabric right away with cold water, and blot dry until no more than a trace of dampness is left. For particularly stubborn marks, a commercial liquid stain remover should give satisfactory results.

75 TREATING HOUSEHOLD STAINS

Wherever it's possible, keep liquid polishes, pens, and cosmetics away from permanent upholstery. Put on lids and shut covers tightly to prevent mishaps. If staining does occur, follow the hints below.

METAL POLISH
Wipe with a sponge wrung out in warm water. Leave to dry, and then brush away any powdery deposit.

SHOE POLISH
Scoop up as much of the polish as you can. Dab the area with a white cloth moistened with turpentine or stain remover. For stubborn marks, treat the stains with denatured alcohol, then rug shampoo.

FOUNTAIN-PEN INK
First, dilute the stain by sponging with clean water. Blot the mark well with paper towels. When dry, treat with commercial stain remover.

NAIL POLISH & LIPSTICK
Use paper tissues to blot up as much of the spill as possible. After testing a hidden area, apply a nonoily nail-polish remover on a soft white cloth.

CANDLE WAX
Do not attempt to pick off the wax. Melt the wax out by placing brown paper over the fabric and heating it with a warm iron. Remove any remaining color traces with denatured alcohol.

CHEWING GUM
Successfully removing soft or hardened gum from permanent upholstery is rarely easy. Try a commercial stain remover, following an initial test, or call in an expert cleaner.

FELT-TIP PEN
Act quickly to prevent the ink from seeping into the fabric. Blot light marks with cotton swabs and larger stains with paper towels. Then dab with denatured alcohol or spray with stain remover.

76 BALLPOINT-PEN MARKS

Act with speed: dried ballpoint-pen marks on fabric – particularly on permanent upholstery, which cannot be washed – are difficult to remove. If the simple treatment shown in the accompanying three steps is unsuccessful, it is advisable to contact the pen's manufacturer for the following information.

- Find out what specific dyes the ballpoint-pen ink contains and what solvents will remove them.
- Ask whether the manufacturer sells its own solvent treatment.
- Check to see whether stains can be removed by a professional cleaner.

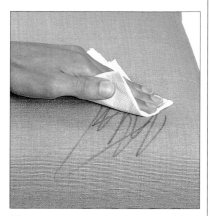

1 △ First, soak up as much of the ink as possible from a small ink mark by pressing a cotton swab into the fabric. Absorb much larger spills by blotting the area with white paper towels.

2 △ Using a new clean cotton swab, gently rub denatured alcohol into the affected area. Be careful while doing so not to spread the color further. Dab repeatedly with fresh cotton swabs until the stain starts to lift.

3 △ If the fabric does not respond to denatured alcohol and color still remains, spray the area with an aerosol stain remover, after an initial test on a hidden section. If this technique fails, get advice from the pen's manufacturer.

77 REMOVING PET HAIR & MUD

If you own a pet, muddy pawprints on armchairs and other furnishings may be a common occurrence – as well as pet hair strewn on cushions or blankets in your pet's favorite sleeping place.

To stop pet hair and mud on their paws from being transferred onto clothing as people are sitting down, follow the advice on this page for their quick removal, repeating as necessary.

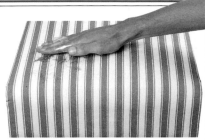

PICKING OFF PET HAIR
Adhesive tape is very effective in picking pet hair off fabric. Wind a length, sticky side out, around three fingers, and then brush the tape over the fabric, picking up hairs until no more adhere. You may need several pieces of tape to finish the job.

1 ◁ Leave the fresh mud to set before tackling it. Then, using a soft brush, lightly sweep up the deposit, being very careful not to damage the upholstery.

2 ▽ Remove any remaining particles of mud with the nozzle attachment on a vacuum cleaner. When every trace of the deposit has been lifted, sponge the upholstery with a weak warm solution of dishwashing liquid. Blot, then dry.

78 SCORCH MARKS ON UPHOLSTERY

Soft furniture can be damaged by tobacco burns. Remove light marks with a solution of equal parts of glycerin and warm water. Leave for two hours and then rinse. Treat severe scorching with 1 tbsp laundry borax to 2 cups (500ml) warm water.

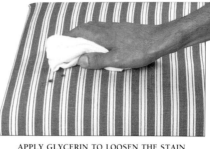

APPLY GLYCERIN TO LOOSEN THE STAIN

79 TREATING BIOLOGICAL STAINS

Urine and vomit are two of the unpleasant stains that are almost inevitable in homes with pets. For hygiene, wear rubber or disposable plastic gloves. Try to scrape or soak up as much of the deposit as you can before thoroughly disinfecting and deodorizing the soiled area.

URINE

Urine can leave a permanent yellow mark and smell if not properly treated. Sponge fresh stains with clear cold water. Blot well, and then dab on a solution of 1 tbsp vinegar to 2 cups (500ml) warm water. Old stains need expert cleaning.

VOMIT

Scoop up any deposit, being careful not to spread the vomit, and then tackle the underlying stain. Sponge the upholstery with warm water containing a few drops of ammonia, then pat dry. Alternatively, use a deodorizing upholstery cleaner.

FECAL STAINS

Wearing disposable plastic gloves, or a plastic bag over your hand, scrape the mess off the upholstery. Remove any remaining traces by sponging the area with a weak solution of warm water and ammonia to disinfect the fabric.

FLOWER POLLEN

Take care to keep flowers such as lilies that have highly colored pollen away from soft furniture. If pollen does happen to get on upholstery, dab the fabric with denatured alcohol, following an initial test. Rinse with a sponge wrung out in warm water.

Lily
pollen
is one of
nature's dyes

BEDS & BEDDING

80 STAINS ON MATTRESSES

Mattress stains need to be treated at once, or the stain will seep through and rot the fabric. Urine and vomit marks are cleared with cold water and dishwashing liquid. Finish off by wiping with cold water and a few drops of antiseptic. Blot well.

Light blood spots do not need wetting: instead, apply a thick paste of baking soda mixed with a little water. When dry, just brush it off. For heavier blood stains, follow the technique in these three steps.

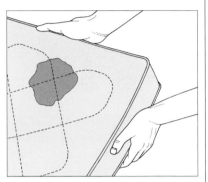

1 △ Take off the bed linen and prop up the mattress on its side (this may take two people) to prevent the stain and any treatment from soaking in.

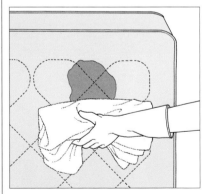

2 △ Wearing rubber gloves, fold up an old towel and place it just beneath the stained area. Press the towel firmly against the mattress to prevent the stain from trickling further down the fabric.

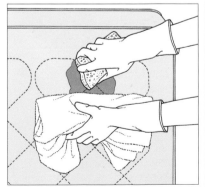

3 △ Sponge the mark with cold salt water until it disappears, and then rinse with clear cold water. Blot the area with paper towels. Leave the mattress on its side to dry after this treatment.

RINSE IN WARM WATER

81 HOT DRINK STAINS ON BLANKETS

If you enjoy drinking hot beverages such as tea, coffee, or cocoa in bed, sooner or later you will probably spill your drink onto the blankets. These stains are a mixture of the coloring from the drink and also grease from the milk, so act quickly to prevent permanent marking.

■ Rinse tea-stained blankets at once in a bucket or bath of warm water. If the mark has dried, try bleaching it carefully with a solution of 1 part hydrogen peroxide to 6 parts water. Rinse and machine-wash.

■ Wash out coffee and cocoa-stained blankets in warm water and machine-wash. Use a commercial stain remover to lift traces of color.

82 STAINS ON PILLOWS & COMFORTERS

You don't have to wash the entire item. Just isolate the immediate area to stop absorption of the spill into the feather or synthetic filling. Hold the stained outer cover and shake down the filling to the other end of the comforter or pillow. Tie string around the sectioned-off area, and soak in a warm enzymatic detergent solution. Rinse the fabric well in clear water, and then leave it to dry naturally.

Tie off the area with string

HOME LAUNDRY

83 TECHNIQUES OF STAIN REMOVAL

A washable garment that has been stained cannot be restored by hot-water washing in a machine. In fact, hot water sets stains, making them almost impossible to remove. Treat the stained item to one, two, or all three of the prewash tips explained below, and regard the machine-wash as a final stage in the stain-removal process.

△ RINSING IN COLD WATER
Act quickly by rinsing the item under cold running water. If you have stained the garment that you are wearing, sponge the mark with cold water until it fades.

△ SOAKING THE FABRIC
If the stain has not faded after rinsing, immerse the fabric in a solution of warm water and enzymatic detergent. Protein stains, such as blood, respond to soaking.

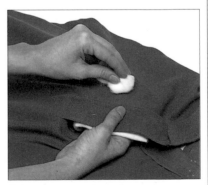

△ SPOT-CLEANING WITH SOLVENT
If stains on washable items remain after soaking, apply a stain solvent before washing. Hold a cloth under the stain to avoid transferring it to another area.

84 LAUNDRY AIDS

Liquid and powdered detergents come in varying strengths, and many contain additives to help remove stains. Some stains require extra treatment from either bleach or laundry borax.

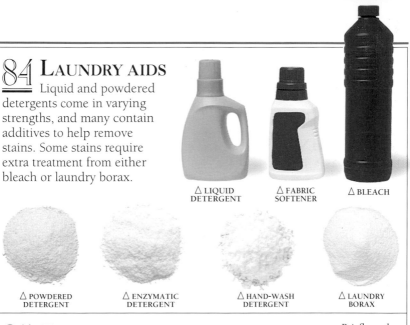

△ LIQUID DETERGENT

△ FABRIC SOFTENER

△ BLEACH

△ POWDERED DETERGENT

△ ENZYMATIC DETERGENT

△ HAND-WASH DETERGENT

△ LAUNDRY BORAX

85 FABRIC TREATMENT

Different types of fabric require different stain treatments. Observe this guide to achieve satisfactory results.

Briefly soak colored items

WHITES
Cotton and other natural fabrics can be bleached, but synthetics may yellow with bleach and respond better to detergent.

COLOREDS
Treat stains gently to prevent fabric from fading. Try soaking in laundry borax – a milder bleaching agent.

NATURAL FABRICS
These can be washed at high temperatures, so rinsing or presoaking the item before washing may be enough to lift stains.

SYNTHETIC FABRICS
Man-made fabrics can be damaged by some chemical stain removers, so test any treatment on a hidden area before use.

DELICATES
Most delicate fabrics require hand-washing and should be treated gently if stained. Avoid strong chemical solvents, and seek expert advice.

86 TREATING FOOD STAINS

During meals, food can all too easily fall onto clothes and table linen. When dealing with light or heavy food spills, first remove the deposit, then treat any grease before turning your attention to the color of the stain. The information on these pages explains how best to treat some of the "difficult" colored food stains without leaving a trace.

CURRY & CURRIED SAUCES
Fresh spills on tablecloths and clothing need to be rinsed in lukewarm water. Rub in a solution of equal parts of glycerin and warm water. Leave for half an hour and then rinse the fabric again. Wash in enzymatic detergent.
- *Bleach persistent stains with a very weak hydrogen peroxide solution.*

CREAM SOUP
Many soups are made from meat or vegetable stock and cream, so this spilled liquid should be treated like grease. Blot up the liquid to limit absorption into the fabric.
- *For delicate fabrics, dab the area with eucalyptus oil, then hand-wash.*
- *For non-delicates, blot the area, and then wash according to the care label instructions to remove residual marks.*

BEETS
Rinse under cold running water. Soak coloreds in a solution made from 1 tbsp laundry borax to 2 cups (500ml) warm water. For whites, cover the stained area with laundry borax powder and pour on hot water.

JAM & JELLY
Scoop up any deposit with a spoon and wipe with a clean damp cloth. Wash fresh stains immediately. Dried-on stains need to be presoaked in a solution made from 1 tbsp laundry borax powder to 2 cups (500ml) clear warm water.

MUSTARD
To loosen fresh stains, first rub the fabric between your fingers in a mild detergent solution. Then, add 1 tsp of ammonia to 2 cups (500ml) of cold water and use this to sponge over the stained area. Wash gently to lift any remaining traces.

YOGURT
Spoon up any surface deposit, and rinse the fabric well in lukewarm water. Then, wash the item according to the care label. Use a liquid stain remover on stubborn marks.
- *Dried stains need a prewash soak in enzymatic detergent.*

CHOCOLATE

Leave the chocolate to set, then scrape it off. Soak and machine-wash the item in an enzymatic detergent if suitable – or wash as usual.

■ Cover stubborn stains with laundry borax powder, and carefully pour hot water through the fabric.

CREAM

Soak up surface liquid spills with paper towels, being careful not to spread the stain any further. Wash the fabric in the hottest water it can withstand.

■ Treat items that cannot bear very hot temperatures with a commercial stain remover before washing.

■ For delicate fabrics, dab the area with a little eucalyptus oil, then gently hand-wash the item.

GRAVY

Blot the area dry with paper towels, then tackle the oily stain by soaking overnight in tepid water, and then deal with any remaining color by washing according to the fabric care label.

■ Dried marks can be lifted by soaking in enzymatic detergent solution. Check the care label before this treatment.

TOMATO SAUCE

Scrape off the thick deposit with a metal spoon, and hold the fabric under cold running water, rubbing it gently between your fingers. Loosen the stain with a pre-wash laundry product then machine-wash in a detergent, according to the care label.

Treat tomato and other thick bottled sauces in the same way

87 DARK-COLORED FRUIT STAINS

Soft, juicy red berries can easily fall on clothes or table linen and, because of their potent color, cause problem stains. Try to treat the stain while it is fresh. Dried stains, discovered hours after the event, can cause permanent soiling unless handled with care.

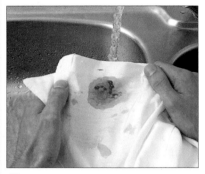

1 △ Remove the item of clothing or table linen, and dilute the stain by rinsing it in the sink under cold running water until most of the mark has lifted.

2 △ Treat any color residue by dabbing the stained area using a soft white cloth dipped in denatured alcohol or a commercial stain remover.

△ NATURAL TREATMENT FOR FRESH STAINS
If you are eating outside or simply do not have any denatured alcohol to hand, rub a cut lemon over the stain: in the sun, lemon juice works as a bleaching agent.

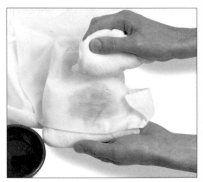

△ HOW TO DEAL WITH DRIED STAINS
First lubricate the dried fruit stain by applying a mixture of glycerin diluted with equal parts of warm water. Leave for one hour, then treat as for fresh stains.

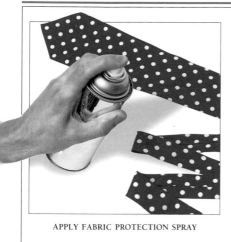

APPLY FABRIC PROTECTION SPRAY

88 GREASE STAINS ON TIES

Ties are particularly susceptible to grease spots, from food and daily handling, but sponging off stains often leaves behind a ring mark. Before putting on a tie, go over it with fabric protection spray. This spray will resist the absorption of grease into the fibers so that there is time to wipe away spills. Carry a small pad impregnated with stain remover or a spare tie in your bag or briefcase for use in emergencies.

89 EGG STAINS

Soft-cooked eggs are easy to slop on clothes and table linen. The first rule is not to sponge off yolk or white of egg with hot water, since this will make the egg congeal. If you do not have time to treat the egg, cover it with a damp cloth to stop it from setting.

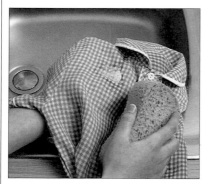

△ SPONGE WITH COLD SALT WATER
Fill a dishpan with cold water, and add about two tablespoons of salt. Sponge the fabric with cold salt water until the egg disappears. Rinse and dry.

△ SOAK IN ENZYMATIC DETERGENT
If the egg stain still remains after the salt-water treatment, soak the washable fabric in enzymatic detergent for a few hours. Rinse, dry, and spray with stain remover.

90 TREATING DRINK STAINS

For washable fabrics, rinsing the item under running water then washing is the rule for removing fresh drink stains. Old stains that have had time to dry on the fabric need a bit more time and attention, but most color traces can still be lifted by soaking or treating fabrics with a stain remover. These hints deal with both new and old stains.

MILK
Rinse fresh stains in tepid water, then wash as usual. When dry, use a liquid stain remover if marks remain.
■ *Presoak dried stains in an enzymatic detergent. A weak hydrogen peroxide solution is the alternative, for all fabrics except nylon.*

FRUIT JUICE DRINKS
Like fresh fruit juice and cola drinks, fruit juice drinks leave behind a sticky colored residue. Treat at once following the method outlined for fruit juice (see right).

LIGHT COFFEE & HOT CHOCOLATE
Rinse thoroughly in warm water. Soak in a warm enzymatic detergent solution, if the fabric is suitable, or try rubbing with a commercial stain-removing bar. Wash as usual. When dry, use a stain remover to lift any traces of stain that may be left.
■ *Treat stubborn marks on white linen and cotton by soaking in a mild solution of bleach.*

Rinse and soak hot chocolate stains very thoroughly

FRUIT JUICE

Dark fruit juices such as cranberry and red grape will often leave behind a stubborn residue of color. Deal with new stains by rinsing them under a cold running tap, then treat with a stain remover.

■ For old stains, soak the fabric in cold water before washing – according to the care label – with a heavy-duty detergent.

BLACK COFFEE

The strong coloring of black coffee should be treated while fresh for successful stain removal. As with light coffee and cocoa, rinse the stained fabric immediately in warm water. Soak the item in an enzymatic detergent, if suitable, and wash as usual. When dry, use a stain remover to lift any traces of color.

COLA DRINKS

These tend to leave behind a very sticky stain as they dry, so wash immediately under cold running water, rubbing between your fingers until as much of the mark as possible has disappeared. Treat any remaining color by dabbing on denatured alcohol or a stain remover.

■ To treat old stains, hold a white cloth under the stain, and dab on a solution of equal parts glycerin and warm water. Leave for one hour, rinse, and treat as for fresh marks, described above.

HARD LIQUOR

The tried-and-tested treatment for hard liquor is the same as that for beer (Tip 92). Fresh stains are simple to lift by rinsing in tepid water, then washing.

■ Dried stains on whites need bleaching with hydrogen peroxide.
■ Sponge coloreds with a solution of vinegar.

PORT & SHERRY

These tend to be stickier than other spilled alcoholic drinks. Rinse the fabric under warm running water while rubbing the fabric between your fingers, then wash according to the care label. If color remains, use a stain remover or denatured alcohol.

Port makes a sticky stain

91 DRIED TEA STAINS

Fresh tea stains disappear when rinsed in lukewarm water, and then soaked in laundry borax, but dried stains need special care.

1 △ Carefully drape the tea-stained item over a dishpan, and then sprinkle with laundry borax powder until there is a thick layer of powder over the stain.

2 △ Slowly pour hot water from a kettle around the perimeter of the stain. Work in a circular motion toward the fabric center. Repeat the treatment, if necessary, before washing as usual.

92 BEER ON CLOTHES

The important point to remember about both major and minor beer stains is that you must act quickly to get the best results.

△ RINSE IN TEPID WATER
Fresh beer and ale stains are quite simple to remove. Thoroughly rinse the stained fabric in tepid water and wash as usual.

△ SPONGE WITH A SOLUTION OF VINEGAR
To remove any remaining traces of beer or ale from colored fabrics, sponge with a solution made from 2 tbsp white vinegar and 2 cups (500ml) of water.

93 RED WINE ON FABRIC

The fibers in most fabrics quickly absorb red wine, so try to mop up the spill with a white paper towel or paper napkin before it has time to seep in. Never use colored napkins since they can transfer dye to the stain. Instead, sprinkle the area with table salt.

△ SPRINKLE WITH SALT
As a quick-action solution, pour salt onto red-wine spills. Salt rapidly absorbs the wine and limits damage to a small area.

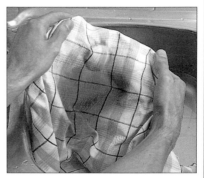

△ RINSE FRESH STAINS IN WARM WATER
Rinse out fresh red-wine stains in warm water. If the stain holds, soak the fabric in laundry borax powder and warm water.

△ SOAK COLORED ITEMS IN DETERGENT
Soak heavily soiled, colored items in a strong detergent solution, then wash as usual. For particularly stubborn stains, try the treatment for tea (Tip 91).

△ BLEACH WASHABLE WOOL AND SILK
Wearing gloves, bleach fresh red-wine stains on white wool or silk in a bucket containing 1 part hydrogen peroxide to 6 parts warm water. Rinse and wash.

94 TREATING PRODUCT STAINS ON FABRIC

Many ordinary products in the house are manufactured from a complex mix of both colored dyes and synthetic compounds. When spills occur on washable fabrics, product stains will usually respond to treatment that is combined with machine-washing. Be careful, since these stains are more difficult to remove from nonwashable items.

FELT-TIP PEN
Absorb as much of the felt-tip pen ink as you can by pressing a paper towel over the marked fabric. Apply denatured alcohol on a cotton swab to the stained area, and then wash with soapflakes: they treat stains of this sort much more effectively than detergent.

MEDICINE
Sticky colored medicine stains should be treated quickly so that they do not set into a solid deposit. Machine-washing should remove most marks, but stubborn stains can be treated with denatured alcohol.
■ *Hold a white cloth under the stained area to stop color from being transferred to the other side of the fabric. Gently dab the affected area with denatured alcohol after testing a hidden part of the fabric.*

METAL POLISH
Wipe with white tissues or paper towels to clear as much of the liquid deposit as possible. Before washing, apply a commercial liquid stain remover. Normal washing should remove leftover traces of polish.

WASHABLE-INK PEN
If ink stains remain after washing, rub persistent marks with half a fresh lemon, or apply fresh lemon juice. Hold a piece of white cloth underneath and on top of the stained area, and press together until most of the color has lifted. Repeat as many times as necessary, and rinse. Wash the item once more according to its fabric and care label.

SHOE POLISH
Light polish marks respond to an aerosol stain remover – or add a few drops of ammonia to the rinsing water during washing. For heavy marks, first lift off deposit – if any – then dab with turpentine before rinsing and washing.

CREOSOTE & TAR
Stains left by creosote and tar are difficult to remove, and particular care needs to be taken not to transfer them onto any other surfaces.
■ *Scrape off the deposit, then place an absorbent white pad on top of the mark. Dab the stained area from below with a cotton ball moistened with a few drops of eucalyptus oil, then wash.*

*Make sure to wash
washable fabrics after
treating any stain*

CANDLE WAX
*On washable
fabrics, use the
same warm-iron
method as for
carpets (Tip 18).
Next, dab on some
denatured alcohol to
take away the color
residue, then wash.*

*Denatured
alcohol can lift
color residue*

DYE STAINS
*Immerse white and colorfast items in an
enzymatic detergent solution just until the
discoloration has disappeared. Wash as
usual according to the care label.*
■ *For fabrics that are not colorfast, soak
in a mild hydrogen peroxide solution for
about 15 minutes and rinse well.*

LATEX PAINT
*Fresh latex paint stains are water-soluble
and, once blotted, the fabric can be
sponged with cold water and washed.
Recently dried paint stains will respond to
a commercial stain remover, but larger
deposits that have already become hard
are best treated by a professional cleaner.*

OIL-BASED PAINT
*Gloss and semigloss paints are oil based,
so stains should be dabbed with turpentine,
after an initial test, to break down the oil.
Next, sponge the area with cold water.
Repeat the whole treatment several times.*
■ *Be patient: wash the fabric only when
you are sure all traces of paint have been
removed. The stain is set once the fabric
has been washed, and will then respond
only to the treatment of a professional.*

95 CHEWING GUM

If you are unlucky enough to sit on a discarded piece of sticky chewing gum, the garment can be restored – without washing – by placing it in a freezer until the gum hardens. This usually works.

1 Put the marked garment in a plastic bag and place it in the freezer for an hour, or until the gum hardens.

2 Remove the item from the freezer, and bend the fabric until the gum cracks. Pick it off with your fingernails.

96 LIPSTICK STAINS

Successfully treat stubborn lipstick marks on clothes, table linen, and bathroom towels by first sponging the affected area using denatured alcohol on a white cloth. Follow this treatment by applying a little undiluted dishwashing liquid onto the stain. Rub it into the fabric with a clean finger, and then wash the item according to the care label.

TREAT WITH DISHWASHING LIQUID
Squirt undiluted dishwashing liquid from the bottle onto the stained area, for an accurate application.

97 BIOLOGICAL STAINS

Adults and children who have active outdoor lives soon manage to stain their clothing with a wealth of biological marks. The pre- and postwash treatments described here will help you get the best results out of your home laundry treatments.

PERSPIRATION
This appears as a yellowish or discolored patch in the armpit area of clothes. Sponge fresh stains with a mild ammonia solution made from 1 tsp ammonia to 2 cups (500ml) cold water, and rinse well.
- *Where perspiration has caused color to run, sponge with 1 tbsp of white vinegar in 1 cup (250ml) of water.*

GRASS STAINS
Most sports shorts are polyester and, when stained, respond to soaking followed by washing in enzymatic detergent. Rub larger marks with a heavy-duty hand-cleaner, and then denatured alcohol. Rinse and wash as usual.

URINE
Rinse colored fabrics in cold water, then wash according to the fabric type: this should remove both odor and yellowing.
- *Treat pale fabrics by bleaching them in a solution of 1 part hydrogen peroxide to 6 parts cold water containing a few drops of ammonia. Alternatively, soak the item in enzymatic detergent (read the care label first) or use a commercial stain remover.*

POLLEN
Normal washing removes light stains on fabrics. If not, dab lightly with denatured alcohol, and then gently sponge off with clean warm water.

BIRD DROPPINGS
Scrape off the deposit and launder washable fabrics. A mild bleach or hydrogen peroxide solution may work with difficult stains on white and pale garments.

VOMIT
Thoroughly rinse the affected area under cold running water until the mark begins to fade. Soak, then wash in enzymatic detergent, or simply wash as usual according to fabric type.

BLOOD
Pour a handful of salt into a bucket of cold water and soak the item in it for 15 minutes before washing according to fabric type and care label.

98 INGRAINED DIRT ON COLLARS & CUFFS

Grime quickly builds up on shirt collars and cuffs, and needs a prewash treatment to prevent the stain from setting during the wash.

To help keep collars and cuffs clean between washes, use ironing spray or spray starch when pressing the freshly laundered garment.

1 Gently rub a bar of moistened soap along the length of the dirty mark. Hair shampoo is an effective substitute.

2 Use a clean toothbrush and water to work up a lather. Rinse and wash the garment when the mark has faded.

Escaping steam is hotter than boiling water

STEAMING OFF RING MARKS

99 REMOVING WATERMARKS

When treating delicate fabrics such as silk or nonwashable items, you often need to dab the fabric with a wet sponge as the final step. Doing this may leave behind a ring mark of water when the fabric dries.

To remove a watermark of this kind, simply bring a kettle of water to the boil: hold the watermarked area of the item in the steam until the ring disappears. Remember to keep your fingers well away from the path of the steam, which could cause you a very painful burn.

100 MARKS ON SUEDE

Greasy substances spilled on suede can leave a permanent stain. Blot the grease with kitchen towel, then rub the area with a block suede cleaner, kept handy. For persistent stains, wrap a cotton pad in a clean cloth, apply a little cigarette lighter fluid to it, and dab the stain, being careful to test a hidden part first.

Carefully dab the stain to remove it

△ **RUBBING OFF DRIED MUD**
Remove traces of dried mud and surface grime from suede shoes by rubbing the dry shoe with a clean white eraser. This technique also helps raise any crushed pile.

◁ **REMOVING HEAVY GREASE**
To deal with heavy grease stains, apply cigarette lighter fluid right onto the problem area. Then treat the whole shoe, if necessary, to avoid a patchy appearance.

101 SOILED CANVAS

Lift surface dirt from canvas shoes by gently scrubbing the fabric with a clean toothbrush dipped in rug shampoo. Sponge away the resultant foam with warm water. For stubborn marks, such as grass stains, use a nail brush dipped in a solution of dishwashing liquid and warm water. Machine-wash the shoes on a low-heat cycle, and let dry naturally.

SHAMPOOING LIGHT MARKS

INDEX

ACKNOWLEDGMENTS

Dorling Kindersley would like to thank Hilary Bird for compiling the index, Fiona Wild for proofreading and editorial help, and Robert Campbell and Mark Bracey for DTP assistance. Thanks also to Modena Merchants Ltd. for bathroom equipment.

Photography
KEY: t *top*; b *bottom*; c *center*; l *left*; r *right*
Andy Crawford 1; 4; 5; 6br; 10; 11tl; 13; 15tl; 17b; 18c; 46; 47t; 33cr; 34cr; 35t; 36; 41tr; 53br; 55t; 62l; 68; 69; 71; Stephen Oliver 25br; Colin Walton 6tl; 7; 9; 11b; 15br; 17tr; 19; 23br; 24br; 25t; 26; 28; 29; 30tr; 31tr; 32br; 33cl; 34bl; 35br; 38; 39t; 40; 41b; 42; 43; 45; 46; 49; 50; 51tr; 53tl; 54; 58; 59; 62r; 63; 66; Matthew Ward 2; 3; 8; 12; 14; 16; 18; 20; 21; 27b; 30br; 31br; 37; 44; 47; 48; 51br; 55br; 56; 57; 60; 61; 64; 65; 67; 72.

Illustrations
Kuo Kang Chen and John Woodcock.